The Paralympics

Nick Hunter

First published in 2011 by Wayland

Copyright © Wayland 2011

This paperback edition published in 2012 by Wayland.

Wayland
338 Euston Road
London NW1 3BH

Wayland Australia
Level 17/207 Kent Street
Sydney, NSW 2000

Produced for Wayland by Calcium
Design: Simon Borrough and Paul Myerscough
Editor: Sarah Eason
Editor for Wayland: Katie Woolley
Picture researcher: Susannah Jayes

British Library Cataloguing in Publication Data

Hunter, Nick.
   The Paralympics. — (The Olympics)
   1. Paralympics—Juvenile literature. 2. Sports for people
   with disabilities—England—London—Juvenile literature.
   I. Title II. Series
   796'.0456-dc22

ISBN: 978 0 7502 7067 0

Printed in China
Wayland is a division of Hachette Children's Books,
an Hachette UK company.
www.hachette.co.uk

The website addresses (URLs) included in this book were
valid at the time of going to press. However, because
of the nature of the internet, it is possible that some
addresses may have changed, or sites may have changed
or closed down since publication. While the author and
Publisher regret any inconvenience this may cause the
readers, no responsibility for any such changes can be
accepted by either the author or the Publisher.

Picture Acknowledgements:

Cover Main image: Shutterstock: Chen Wei Seng.
Inset images: Shutterstock: Radu Razvan tl,
John Kropewnicki tr, Alistair Scott bl, Lucian Coman br,
Spine image: Shutterstock: Chen Wei Seng. Back cover
image: Dreamstime: Shariff Che' Lah.
Pages Corbis: Hulton-Deutsch Collection 6; Dreamstime:
Carmentianya 2, 4, 27, 28, Davewebbphoto 7, 24, Shariff
Che' Lah 1, 21, 22, 23, Screengreen 18, Michael Sheehan
16b, Anke Van Wyk 19, Jian Zhang 5; Getty Images: 8–9, 13,
17, 20, 25, AFP 15, 26, 29; London 2012: 11; Shutterstock:
Chen Wei Seng 10, 12, 14, 16c.

Contents

Paralympics 2012

On 29 August 2012, thousands of **elite** athletes will parade through London's Olympic Stadium at the opening ceremony of the Paralympic Games. A flame will be lit in the Stadium. On behalf of all the other athletes, one competitor will take an **oath** to follow the rules of the Games. All the athletes at this opening ceremony will have overcome challenging **disabilities** and trained for years to compete against the very best in their chosen sport.

In 2008, the US men's team set a new Paralympic record by winning the 4 x 100 metres event in 42.75 seconds.

WORD FILE

The word 'Paralympic' was originally a combination of the word 'paraplegic' (which means paralysed from the waist down) and 'Olympic'. As athletes with other disabilities joined the **Paralympic Movement**, the word came to mean 'parallel' and 'Olympic' because the Paralympic and **Olympic Movement** work side by side.

What is the Paralympics?

The Paralympics is the biggest sporting event for the world's best athletes with disabilities. They are held every four years and include different sports in which athletes compete against others with similar disabilities.

The London Paralympics in 2012 will begin just 17 days after the Olympic Games end. Since the Paralympics in Seoul, South Korea, in 1988, cities that bid to **host** the Olympic Games also host the Paralympics in the same year. The Winter Paralympics also take place every four years following the Winter Olympics. The previous Winter Paralympics took place in Vancouver, Canada, in 2010 and the next Winter Paralympics will begin in Sochi, Russia, on 7 March 2014.

Paralympic athletes circle the Stadium in front of the crowd during the opening ceremony in Beijing in 2008.

How the Paralympics began

The Paralympic story began during the Second World War (1939–1945), when Dr Ludwig Guttmann founded the National **Spinal Injuries** Centre at Stoke Mandeville Hospital in the UK. The centre was created to care for soldiers who had suffered spinal injuries during the war. Sport was used as part of the patients' treatment and for relaxation. In 1948, a sporting competition called the Stoke Mandeville Games was held at the hospital and organised to coincide with the staging of the Olympic Games in London.

Olympic insights

The first Stoke Mandeville Games began on the same day as the London Olympics in 1948. In its very first event, 16 servicemen and women with spinal injuries competed in an archery competition.

After the Stoke Mandeville Games, wheelchair sports such as basketball became recognised as competitive events as well as a means to **rehabilitate** injured soldiers.

The Paralympics continue

The Stoke Mandeville Games were held again in 1952. This time, athletes with disabilities from the Netherlands competed against Stoke Mandeville patients. Then, in 1960, athletes from around the world took part in the first official international games for athletes with disabilities. The event took place in Rome, two weeks after the Olympic Games had been held there. These were later named as the first ever Paralympic Games. Ever since, the Games have taken place in the same year as the Olympics.

Expansion

The popularity of the event grew and the Toronto Paralympics in 1976 were much bigger than previous Games.

Visually-impaired athletes and people with other disabilities competed for the first time in 1976. Later in the same year, the first Winter Paralympics took place in Sweden. Sports included skiing, skating and **ice-sledge** racing. Many new events have been added since the 1976 Toronto Games, to both the Summer and Winter Paralympics. Today, Paralympic sports range from sailing and **powerlifting** to wheelchair basketball and football.

Olympics by numbers

14 men and **2** women took part in the 1948 Stoke Mandeville Games
400 athletes from **23** countries competed at the 1960 Paralympic Games
198 athletes from **16** countries took part in the first Winter Paralympics in Örnsköldsvik, Sweden, in 1976
3,057 athletes took part in **732** events at the 1988 Paralympic Games in Seoul, South Korea
3,951 athletes from **146** countries took part in the 2008 Paralympics

Alpine skiing, or downhill skiing, was one of the sports that featured at the 2010 Paralympics in Vancouver, Canada.

The Paralympic Movement

The Paralympic Movement includes more than 160 National Paralympic Committees from different countries and governing bodies of Paralympic sports. The **International Paralympic Committee (IPC)** organises the Summer and Winter Paralympic Games and leads the Paralympic Movement from its base in Bonn, Germany. The IPC was formed in 1989.

Organising the Games

The Paralympic Movement and the IPC are totally separate from the **International Olympic Committee (IOC)** which organises the Olympic Games. However, the organisations work closely together to make the Olympic and Paralympic Games happen and the IOC decides where the Olympics and Paralympics will be staged.

One athlete from each nation represented at the Paralympics carries their country's flag around the Stadium at the opening ceremony.

Olympic insights

The Paralymic **anthem** and lyrics (song words) were completed in 2001. The anthem is called 'Hymn de l'avenir', which means 'Anthem of the Future'. It is played during the Paralympic opening ceremony as the Paralympic flag is raised.

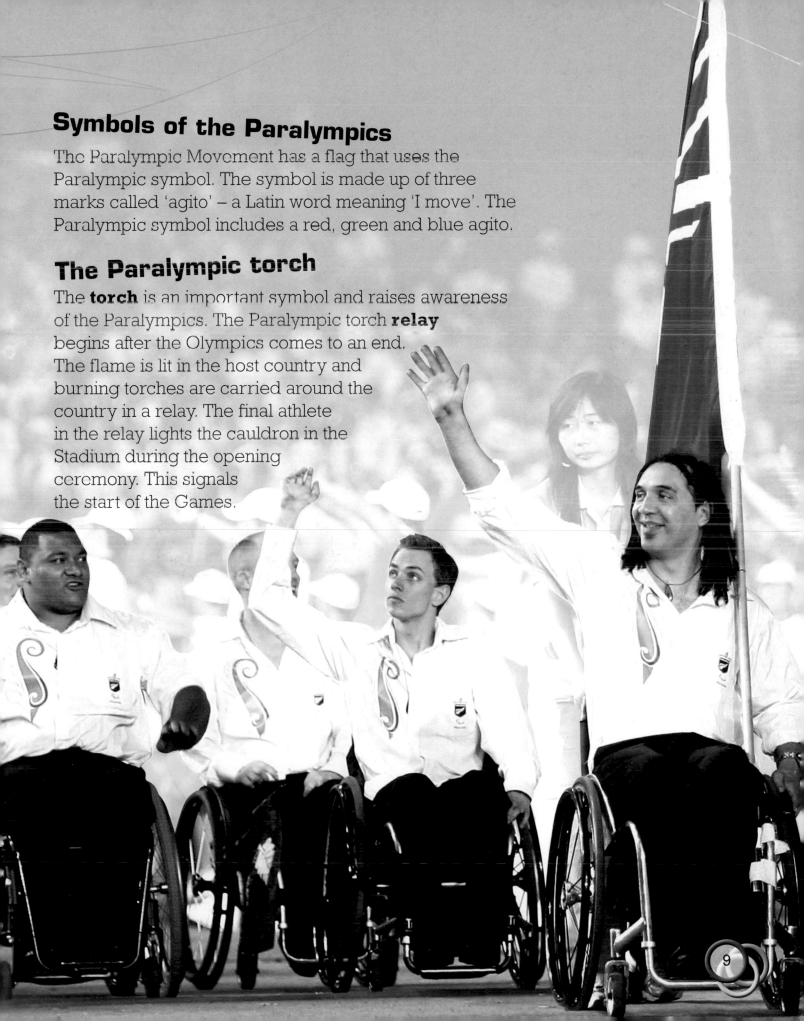

Symbols of the Paralympics

The Paralympic Movement has a flag that uses the Paralympic symbol. The symbol is made up of three marks called 'agito' – a Latin word meaning 'I move'. The Paralympic symbol includes a red, green and blue agito.

The Paralympic torch

The **torch** is an important symbol and raises awareness of the Paralympics. The Paralympic torch **relay** begins after the Olympics comes to an end. The flame is lit in the host country and burning torches are carried around the country in a relay. The final athlete in the relay lights the cauldron in the Stadium during the opening ceremony. This signals the start of the Games.

Making the Paralympics happen

Whilst London has hosted the Olympic Games on two previous occasions in 1908 and 1948, 2012 will be the very first time it has hosted the Paralympics. The team organising the London Olympics has promised to ensure that the 2012 preparations will include some of the best Paralympic facilities in Olympic history.

Building the Paralympics

Many new sporting **venues** have been built for the London Olympics and Paralympics. Planners need to ensure that all these venues are suitable not just for disabled **spectators** but also for the athletes competing at the Paralympics. Many of these venues will be in the Olympic Park in Stratford, east London.

Paralympic table tennis champions, such as Natalia Partyka of Poland, will compete at London's ExCel Exhibition Centre in 2012.

"We want to set new standards on and off the track, and be a catalyst for continued change for public attitudes towards disability.
Lord Sebastian Coe, speaking about the London Organising Committee's intentions for the 2012 Paralympic Games.

10

Olympic Park venues and the sports that will take place there are:

Aquatics Centre: swimming.
Basketball Arena: wheelchair basketball, wheelchair rugby.
Eton Manor: wheelchair tennis.
Hockey Centre: five-a-side and seven-a-side football.
Olympic Stadium: athletics, opening and closing ceremonies.
Velodrome: track cycling.

Other venues

The remainder of the Paralympic venues, such as the ExCel Exhibition Centre, will be in locations just 15 minutes away from the Park. The planning behind the 2012 Games has ensured that they will be one of the most compact Games ever, minimising travel times and disruption for Paralympians.

Olympic Village

Paralympic athletes will stay in apartments in the specially built Olympic Village. Like all areas of the Olympic Park, the Olympic Village needs to be accessible for athletes with disabilities. It will be equipped with lifts and wheelchair ramps, and **Braille** and **audio information** will also be available for all visually-impaired athletes.

The Olympic Park has been designed with wide walkways to make access to all areas easy for athletes using wheelchairs.

Paralympic athletes

Athletes from 160 different countries will compete at the London Paralympics. The most successful nation at the Beijing Paralympics in 2008 was China with 89 gold medals, followed by Great Britain with 42 golds and the USA with 36 golds. In 2008, several countries sent athletes to the Paralympics for the first time, including Burundi, Haiti and Georgia.

Different disabilities

The Paralympic Games include athletes with many different disabilities. In order to make the competition fair, a complex system is used to determine which athletes compete against each other. This classification includes five main groups for athletes: spinal injuries, amputees, visually-impaired athletes, those with cerebral palsy and a group called 'les autres', which covers other physical disabilities.

The Paralympics feature athletic events such as track running, the marathon, shot put and high jump.

WORD FILE

amputee: someone who has lost a limb or limbs

cerebral palsy: a condition caused by brain damage before birth that makes a person suffer spasms of their muscles and jerky movements

classification: a method by which athletes are sorted into groups according to their disability. The system ensures that only athletes with similar disabilities compete against each other

Paralympic sports

There will be a total of 20 different sports at the London Paralympics. Some of these sports, such as wheelchair basketball for players with spinal injuries and five a-side football for the visually-impaired, are for athletes with only one type of disability. Other sports, such as swimming and running, include events for athletes with many different types of disability. Athletics is the biggest sport at the Paralympics, with 1,100 athletes taking part in the events in the Olympic Stadium at the 2012 Paralympic Games.

French athlete Laurent Francois was awarded the gold medal in the men's fencing competition at the 2008 Paralympic Games in Beijing.

Olympic insights

Whereas some sports are versions of Olympic events, boccia appears only at the Paralympics. The sport is played in more than 50 countries by athletes with severe cerebral palsy. Similar to lawn bowls, the object of boccia is to roll a ball to finish as close as possible to a target ball.

Olympics by numbers

740 men and **360** women will compete in the athletics programme at the 2012 Paralympic Games. They will be chasing **170** gold medals.

Track and field

London's Olympic Stadium will be full of cheering spectators who have come to watch the Paralympic athletics events. Competitors will race over a variety of distances, from 100-metre and 200-metre sprints to middle-distance runs (such as the 800 metres) and long-distance competitions including the 42,195-metre marathon. They will also compete in jumping and throwing events, such as the long jump and javelin throwing. Athletics is open to all five disability groups (see page 12).

Technology and techniques

The wheelchairs used by Paralympians are very different from wheelchairs for everyday use. They are made from very light materials and, in many cases, have just three wheels to make them more streamlined and therefore faster.

Amputees use artificial or **prosthetic limbs** to run. These are made from light materials, such as plastic and **carbon fibre**, in order to allow the athlete to move as quickly and as freely as possible. Many prosthetic limbs are designed on a computer using a model of the athlete in order to ensure a perfect fit.

In jumping events, athletes are given the signal to jump by a device that makes a sound or by a person who calls to the jumper.

Visually-impaired runners, such as these relay runners, use a sighted guide (centre) to help them run and to receive the relay baton.

Champion runner Oscar Pistorius

South Africa's Oscar Pistorius is one of the best-known Paralympic champions. He won gold medals in his class at 100 metres, 200 metres and 400 metres at the Paralympics in 2008. Pistorius was born with a condition that meant both of his lower legs were so badly deformed that they had to be amputated below the knee when he was a baby. He now runs on curved, artificial feet called 'Cheetah Flex-Feet', which are made of wood and carbon fibre. In 2008, Pistorius won a battle in court for his right to compete at the Olympic Games alongside able bodied athletes, but the verdict did not come in time for him to enter the 2008 Games. He hopes to compete at the 2012 Games instead.

Olympic insights

Oscar Pistorius is not the only Paralympian who has tried to compete at the Olympics. Visually-impaired Paralympic athlete Marla Runyan was allowed to compete and made the final of the women's 1,500 metres at the Sydney Olympics in 2000, finishing eighth. She also won five Paralympic gold medals in 1992 and 1996 in sprint events, the long jump and **pentathlon**.

Oscar Pistorius is nicknamed 'blade runner' because of his extraordinarily fast speeds on the running track.

Paralympic swimming

At the 2012 Paralympic Games, 600 athletes will compete in 148 medal events due to take place over 10 days at London's newly-built Aquatics Centre. Swimming is one of the most popular and oldest of Paralympic sports – it has been part of the Games since they first took place in Rome in 1960.

In the water, Paralympians can often move with a speed and freedom they cannot achieve on land. This makes swimming a very popular Paralympian sport.

South African swimmer Kevin Paul took the gold in the 100-metre swim at the Beijing Paralympics in 2008. He achieved a speed of one minute and 8.58 seconds — smashing the world record.

Paralympic rules

The main difference between Olympic and Paralympic swimming is that Paralympic swimmers are allowed to start in the water as well as diving into the pool from starting blocks. Four strokes are used in Paralympic swimming: **freestyle** (front crawl), backstroke, **butterfly stroke** and breaststroke.

Champion swimmer Natalie du Toit

South Africa's Natalie du Toit is one of the greatest ever Paralympic swimmers. She always loved swimming and when she lost her leg in an accident in 2001, she took up Paralympic swimming. Natalie won five gold medals in freestyle, butterfly and **individual medley** at both the Athens and Beijing Paralympics. She hopes to win more in London. In 2008, du Toit competed alongside able-bodied swimmers in the Olympic 10-kilometre open water swim, finishing in sixteenth place. Her ambition is to finish in the top five in this event at the London Olympics.

Visually-impaired swimmers have an assistant, called a 'tapper', who taps the swimmer to tell them they are reaching the end of the pool.

Cycle racers

Road cycling first appeared at the 1984 Paralymics, but track cycling made its debut only in 1996. The first cycling events at the Paralympics featured only visually-impaired athletes. New technologies have meant that athletes with other disabilities can now compete on a range of different cycles.

Bikes for disabilities

Paralympic cyclists use different equipment depending on their disability. Cyclists with cerebral palsy use regular bikes, as do some amputee cyclists. Visually-impaired cyclists ride **tandem** bicycles with a guide, and athletes with severe lower-limb disabilities use tricycles, which they power with their arms and hands.

Cycling events

Athletes from different disability groups compete against each other in the road events, which include a road race and a time trial against the clock. Track cycling events include sprints in which visually-impaired tandem cyclists compete in a three-race event and the team with the best overall time wins.

Time trials are also featured in track cycling events. In these races, each cyclist competes to achieve the fastest speed over a set distance. The individual pursuits are races in which two cyclists or two tandem teams start the race on opposite sides of the track. They must then cycle as fast as they can to try to catch the other cyclist or team.

Cyclists with spinal disabilities use handcycles, which they power by turning the wheels with their arms.

After injury

Disabled sport can be very important in rehabilitating those who have been injured in accidents or in war. Jon-Allan Butterworth lost his left arm while serving in the British Royal Airforce (RAF) during the war in Iraq in 2007. Just a few months after having a prosthetic arm fitted, Jon-Allan decided to get involved in disability sport. He took up track cycling and developed his skills to become an elite athlete. He set a world record in 2010 and is hoping to claim gold at the London Paralympics in 2012.

Olympic insights

Spanish cyclist Javier Ochoa was a Tour de France cyclist before being hit by a car while out training with his twin brother Ricardo. Ricardo was killed in the accident but Javier survived. He remained in a coma for several days due to serious head and chest injuries. He recovered and became a Paralympic cyclist, winning gold in the road race at the Athens Paralympics in 2004.

A sighted cyclist rides at the front of a tandem bicycle to guide the visually-impaired cyclist.

Team sports

Paralympic team sports are often specifically designed for athletes with certain types of disability, such as goalball for visually-impaired players. Some Paralympic team sports, such as rowing, are very similar to their Olympic equivalents. Others, such as wheelchair rugby, were created just for athletes with a disability.

Goalball

A ball that contains bells is used in goalball, so that visually-impaired players can hear where the ball is as it moves around the court. Players throw, rather than kick, the ball into a net to score a goal. The goalball spectators and players must remain silent during play so that each team can locate the ball. Both goalball and five-a-side players must wear eyeshades during the match to ensure that players with only partially-impaired eyesight do not have an advantage.

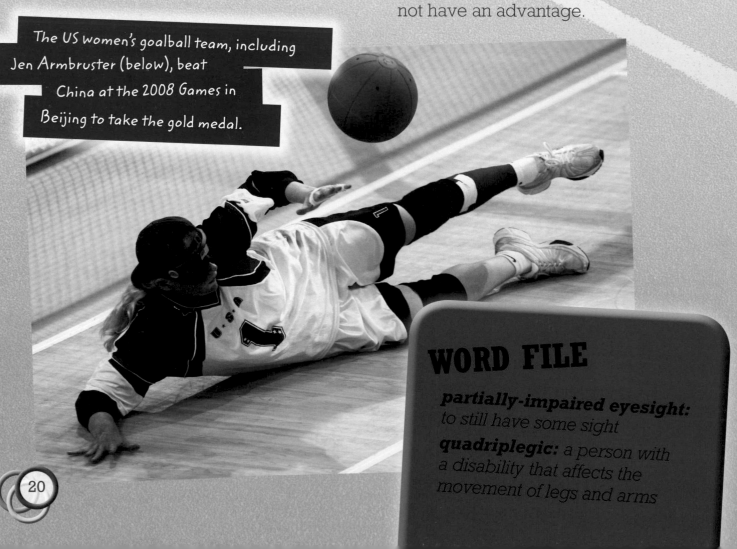

The US women's goalball team, including Jen Armbruster (below), beat China at the 2008 Games in Beijing to take the gold medal.

WORD FILE

partially-impaired eyesight: to still have some sight

quadriplegic: a person with a disability that affects the movement of legs and arms

Football

There are two types of football at the Paralympics, five-a-side and seven-a-side football. Athletes who are visually-impaired play five-a-side football using a ball fitted with a device that makes a sound when it moves. Seven-a-side football is for players with cerebral palsy. Its rules are similar to those of Olympic football, but players throw, rather than kick, the ball into the net.

Basketball

Wheelchair basketball is the fastest growing sport for athletes with disabilities. Athletes with different levels of disability compete. To make games fair, each player is given a points value, depending on the seriousness of his or her disability, with a lower number for a more serious disability. The total points for all players in the team must not be more than 14.

Wheelchair rugby

Wheelchair rugby was invented as an alternative to wheelchair basketball for quadriplegic athletes with limited use of arms and legs. It is a tough sport in which contact between wheelchairs is common, and so was originally called 'murderball'. Teams of four players compete to carry a ball across a goal line. The sport is played on a basketball court and combines elements of basketball, handball and ice hockey.

Wheelchairs for basketball are made from titanium – a hard but light metal. They have a bar, called a footplate, at the front of the chair which protects the players' feet.

Olympic insights

Rowing is the newest team sport at the Paralympics. The first medals in Paralympic rowing were awarded in Beijing in 2008. The sport requires upper body strength and endurance as well as teamwork. Paralympic sailing includes events for individuals and teams of two or three sailors. This sport will be held at Weymouth and Portland on the south coast of the UK in 2012.

Venues and sports

The Paralympic events of 2012 will be taking place in many different venues across east London. Wheelchair tennis will be played at Eton Manor in the Olympic Park. The ExCeL Exhibition Centre in London's Docklands will host combat sports and table tennis, and the Royal Artillery Barracks in Woolwich will host Paralympic archery and shooting.

Racket sports

Wheelchair tennis tests athletes' skill, fitness and speed around the court. The size of the court and equipment used is the same as for able-bodied tennis, but in wheelchair tennis the ball is allowed to bounce twice. In Paralympic table tennis, athletes in wheelchairs compete alongside standing players.

Combat sports

In Paralympic fencing, athletes' wheelchairs are fixed to a frame to stop them moving or falling over during play. Fencers aim to hit their opponents without being touched themselves.

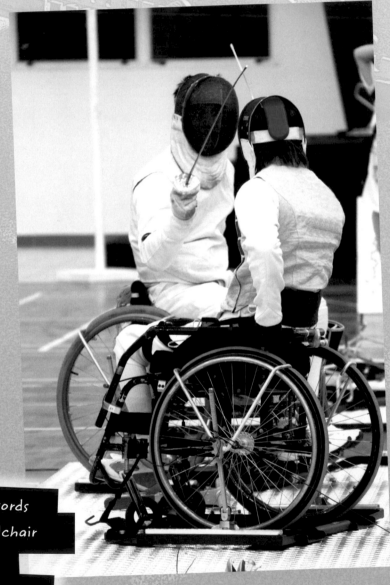

Paralympic fencers hold their swords with one hand and their wheelchair with the other to help them keep their balance during lunges.

Judo for visually impaired judokas (players) is the only martial art at the Paralympics. Each match lasts for five minutes and the winner is the judoka who scores the most points. Competitors are given points for the ability with which they carry out moves. The highest point awarded is for an ippon, meaning 'one full point', a move in which the opponent is thrown onto their back and pinned on the floor for 30 seconds.

Aiming high

Wheelchair sports, such as archery and shooting, test accuracy and concentration. Archery was one of the sports that featured at the first Stoke Mandeville Games in 1948.

Champion player Esther Vergeer

Few Paralympians or Olympians have dominated their sport like Esther Vergeer of the Netherlands. Vergeer has been the world's number one wheelchair tennis player for more than 10 years and won Paralympic gold medals in 2000, 2004 and 2008. Vergeer, who lost the use of her legs during an operation on her spine when she was eight, is one of the most successful and enduring Paralympians.

> " At the beginning, it was all about disability and overcoming obstacles... but I just want to be seen as someone who is living for their sport... that's the biggest compliment you can have as an athlete. "
>
> Esther Vergeer, three-times Paralympic tennis gold medallist.

Archers aim at a circular target marked with 10 rings. A hit in the central ring scores 10 points, with decreasing points for every ring outside it.

Winter Paralympics

The first Winter Paralympic events were held in Sweden in 1976 and included skiing for athletes who had lost limbs and visually-impaired athletes. The range of sports has since expanded and athletes from all disability groups now compete.

Vancouver 2010

In 2010, the Winter Paralympics were held in Vancouver, Canada. The five sports included were alpine skiing, cross-country skiing, **ice-sledge hockey**, wheelchair **curling** and **biathlon**, which combines skiing and shooting. Sound signals tell visually-impaired athletes where the target is during the shooting part of the biathlon competition, so that athletes can aim accurately.

Ice-sledge hockey

One of the fastest and toughest of Paralympic sports is ice-sledge hockey, which is much like ice hockey played by able-bodied athletes. Instead of skates, players use sledges to move around the ice. They use sticks with one pointed end to push themselves along and an end with a blade for hitting a disc, called a puck, towards the goal. For many local fans, this sport was the highlight of the Vancouver Paralympics, and they expected a Canadian victory. Fans were shocked when Canada was knocked out of the semi-finals by Japan and the gold medal was won by the USA.

Ice-sledge hockey is played by Paralympic athletes with a lower-body disability.

Canada's skiing star

Alpine skier Lauren Woolstencroft first competed at the Salt Lake City Winter Olympics in 2002, where the Canadian won her first gold medals. When the Paralympics came to her home country in 2010, she won five gold medals in the skiing competitions. Although she was born without legs below her knees and no left arm below the elbow, Woolstencroft began skiing at the age of four on her prosthetic limbs.

> " It kind of hit me at the right time, and once I tried skiing racing, I instantly fell in love with it. "
>
> Lauren Woolstencroft, speaking about her first alpine skiing competition at the age of 14.

Lauren won her fifth gold medal at the 2010 Games. She set a new record of the most gold medals ever won by an athlete at the Winter Paralympics.

Paralympic controversies

Some of the sporting issues that are associated with the Olympics have also affected the Paralympics, including drug-taking and classification problems. Like the Olympic Movement, the Paralympic Movement will be working hard to overcome these issues at the 2012 Games.

Use of drugs

The illegal use of drugs, or doping, by athletes to increase their performance is a problem in many areas of top-level sport. The Paralympics are no exception and at least 1,000 drug tests will be carried out at the 2012 Paralympics. Doping can lead to sporting bans for the athletes and long-term health problems.

Powerlifting is one of the sports most commonly associated with drug-taking in both the Olympics and Paralympics.

Rules of entry

The classification of athletes in the Paralympics can also cause problems. In order for athletes to compete, organisers have to decide how their disabilities should be classified. This has led to a few athletes arriving at the Paralympics to be told that their disability is not severe enough for them to compete or they did not fit into any of the classification categories. This is heartbreaking for athletes. At the 2008 Games, British athlete Rebecca Chin came second in the women's discus event only to be told that she no longer qualified following complaints from other athletes that her cerebral palsy disability was not severe enough.

Caught on court

One of the biggest Paralympic scandals was uncovered after the 2000 Paralympics in Sydney, Australia. Several members of the Spanish basketball team for athletes with learning disabilities were found to have no disability at all. Since then, learning disabilities have been removed from the Paralympics because of the great difficulty in policing this issue.

Olympic insights

Media coverage of the Paralympics has increased greatly over the years. However, there is often criticism about the amount and type of media coverage. Some athletes complain that media coverage often focuses on the athletes overcoming their disability, rather than just presenting them as elite athletes.

Paralympians have worked hard to be recognised for their sporting abilities, not their disabilities.

The London Paralympics

When the Paralympic flame is lit to begin the London Games, it will mark the end of many years of preparation. New venues and transport links are only part of the story. For Paralympic athletes, the London Paralympics will be their moment on the world stage after years of training.

Changing attitudes

The number of athletes taking part and the number of sports at the Paralympics has increased over recent years. This has made competitions much tougher and winning a medal even harder. As a result, there has been a change in attitude to the Paralympics as the public have become more aware of the skill and commitment needed to succeed at the Games.

China's Ting Zhang (front) and her team's disciplined training helped them to win the women's 4 x 100 metres at the Beijing Games. They also set a new world record of three minutes and 36.11 seconds.

Inspiring champions

The London Paralympics in 2012 will give competitors such as British swimmer Eleanor Simmonds the chance to inspire the next generation of Paralympians.

Eleanor first started swimming at the age of four and was later inspired by the success of the great British swimmer Nyree Lewis at the 2004 Paralympics. Eleanor began training nine times a week at her local swimming pool for two hours each time. Her natural ability and dedicated training shaped her into a world-class swimmer and, in 2008, she won a gold medal in the women's 200- and 400-metre events at the 2008 Beijing Paralympics. Aged just 13, Eleanor became Britain's youngest Paralympian to ever win a gold medal.

In 2009, when she was just 14, Eleanor was given a **Member of the Order of the British Empire (MBE)** for her achievements at the Paralympics, making her the youngest person to ever receive the award! Eleanor has no doubt inspired many young people to take up swimming and she will be hoping to do even better in front of a home crowd in 2012.

Eleanor won the 2008 women's 400 metres in a spectacular five minutes and 41.34 seconds — creating a new Paralympic record.

> *Better to get a sore neck from aiming too high than a hunchback from aiming too low!*
> Ellie Cole, Australian Paralympic swimmer and three-times-medallist at the Beijing Games in 2008.

Paralympic legends

The London Paralympics will feature many of the greatest Paralympic athletes of all time. Some of them are featured throughout this book. Here are some more Paralympic legends past and present.

Baroness Tanni Grey-Thompson
Born with **spina bifida**

Born in 1969 in Cardiff, Wales, Tanni Grey-Thompson is Britain's greatest ever Paralympian. She won 11 gold medals at four Paralympics from 1992 to 2004 in wheelchair athletics races from 100 to 800 metres. Grey-Thompson also excelled at longer distances, winning the London Marathon six times. Since retiring from athletics in 2007, Grey-Thompson continues to be an active member of the Paralympic Movement and a strong voice in disabled sport. She was made Baroness Grey-Thompson in 2010.

Jonas Jacobsson
Paralysed from the waist down

Born in Sweden in 1965, Jacobsson has an amazing record in the Paralympic shooting competition. At Beijing in 2008, he won three gold medals to bring his total tally to 16 golds in a career that stretches back to the 1980 Paralympics.

Daniel Dias
Born with **malformed** limbs

Born in Campinas, Brazil, in 1988, Daniel Dias did not discover Paralympic swimming until the age of 16, when he saw the 2004 Athens Paralympics on television. He started training and won his first titles at the 2006 International Paralympic Committee (IPC) world championships for swimming. In 2008, Dias won nine Paralympic medals and in 2009 was named World Sportsperson of the Year with a Disability.

Louise Sauvage
Born with **myelodysplasia**

Louise Sauvage was born in 1973 in Perth, Australia, with myelodysplasia. The condition made it difficult for Louise to control her lower body. Her nine gold medals as a Paralympic wheelchair athlete from 1992 to 2000 raised the profile of Paralympic sports in Australia. In 2000, Sauvage lit the Paralympic flame at the start of the Sydney Games.

Glossary

anthem a song that is linked to people or an event, such as the Paralympics

audio information spoken information

biathlon an event in which skiers carry a rifle during a cross-country race and stop to shoot at a target during the race

Braille letters that can be felt by visually impaired readers so that they can read them

butterfly stroke a swimming stroke in which both arms are lifted out of the water at the same time

carbon fibre light, strong material

curling a sport in which competitors have to push a large stone along a sheet of ice towards a target

disabilities conditions that prevent people from doing certain things

elite the best of any group

freestyle a swimming discipline in which the front crawl stroke is used

host to stage or organise an event

ice-sledge a sledge that is used to travel across ice

ice-sledge hockey a Paralympic sport similar to ice hockey in which athletes use sledges to move around

individual medley a race in which all four swimming strokes are used

International Olympic Committee (IOC) the organisation that leads the Olympic Movement and oversees the organisation of the Olympic Games

International Paralympic Committee (IPC) the organisation that leads the Paralympic Movement and oversees the Paralympic Games

malformed not properly formed

Member of the Order of the British Empire an award given by the Queen in recognition of someone's achievements

myelodysplasia a condition that causes severe anaemia (low-iron in the blood) and multiple health problems

oath a promise

Olympic Movement the name for all the groups involved in planning the Olympics

Paralympic Movement the name for all the groups involved in planning the Paralympics

pentathlon an event that includes five different track and field disciplines

powerlifting weightlifting in which a weight is lifted in three or four attempts

prosthetic limbs artificial arms or legs

rehabilitate to restore someone to physical fitness after injury or illness

relay a race in which members of a team each cover part of the total distance

spectators people watching an event

spina bifida a severe spinal condition that can cause paralysis

spinal injuries injuries affecting the spinal cord in the back

tandem a bicycle with seats for two riders

torch a hand-held object with a light or flame at one end

venues buildings or locations where something happens. Each Olympic sport takes place in a particular venue

visually-impaired a disability affecting the eyes and a person's ability to see

Further information

Books

British Olympians (21st Century Lives) by Debbie Foy (Wayland, 2009)

Paralympic Sports Events (Winter Olympic Sports) by Robin Johnson (Crabtree, 2009)

Tanni Grey-Thompson (Sports Files) by John Townsend (Raintree, 2009)

Websites

The International Paralympic Committee's website includes lots of information on Paralympic sports, athletes and the Paralympic Games. Find it at: **www.paralympic.org**

Visit the International Paralympic Committee to discover more about the Games: **www.abilityvability.co.uk**

Index